L'HISTOIRE DE BABAR

le petit éléphant

texte de
Jean de Brunhoff

Musique de
Francis Poulenc

pour Récitant et Piano

Couverture de Laurent de Brunhoff

Dureé 22 minutes

Chester Music

T0159747

Visit Hal Leonard Online at
www.halleonard.com

Contact us:
Hal Leonard
7777 West Bluemound Road
Milwaukee, WI 53213
Email: info@halleonard.com

In Europe, contact:
Hal Leonard Europe Limited
42 Wigmore Street
Marylebone, London, W1U 2RN
Email: info@halleonardeurope.com

In Australia, contact:
Hal Leonard Australia Pty. Ltd.
4 Lentara Court
Cheltenham, Victoria, 3192 Australia
Email: info@halleonard.com.au

First Published in 1949,
Reprinted 1957, 1964, 1969, 1974,
1978, 1983, 1987, 1989, 1993,
1994, 1995, 1997, 1999, 2001

Pour mes petits cousins:

Sophie
Sylvie
Benoit } Périer
Florence
Delphine

Yvan
Alain } Villotte
Marie-Christine
Margueritte-Marie

et mes petits amis

Marthe Bosredon
André Lecoeur

en souvenir de Brive

FRANCIS POULENC
1940

NOTE

An English translation* will be found
on a loose leaf at the end of this copy,
and will be supplied to all countries
except the United States of America,
and Canada.

Copies of the music with French
words only may be used in all countries of the world.

Orchestral version by Jean Francaix, available on hire

HISTOIRE DE BABAR
le petit éléphant

Récit de
Jean de Brunhoff

Musique de
Francis Poulenc

Le récitant annoncera le titre de l'oeuvre et le nom des auteurs.

Dans la grande forêt un petit éléphant est né. Il s'appelle Babar. Sa maman l'aime beaucoup.
Pour l'endormir, elle le berce avec sa trompe, en chantant tout doucement.

Babar a grandi. Il joue maintenant avec les autres enfants éléphants. C'est un des plus gentils. Il s'amuse à creuser le sable avec un coquillage.

Babar se promène très heureux sur le dos de sa maman.

Tout à coup un vilain chasseur, caché

derrière un buisson, tire sur eux.

Le chasseur a tué la maman. Les singes se cachent, les oiseaux s'envolent. Le chasseur court pour attraper le pauvre Babar. Babar se sauve parce qu'il a peur du chasseur.

Molto agitato

6

Au bout de quelques jours, bien fatigué, il arrive près d'une ville. . . . Il est très étonné parce que c'est la première fois qu'il voit tant de maisons — que de choses nouvelles! ces belles avenues! Ces autos et ces autobus!

Pourtant ce qui intéresse le plus Babar, ce sont deux messieurs qu'il rencontre dans la rue. Il pense: ''Vraiment ils sont très biens habillés. Je voudrais bien avoir aussi un beau costume . . . Mais comment faire?

Heureusement, une vieille dame très riche, qui aimait beaucoup les petits éléphants, comprend en le regardant qu'il a envie d'un bel habit. Comme elle aime faire plaisir, elle lui donne son porte-monnaie.

Babar lui dit: ''Merci, Madame''.

8

Maintenant Babar habite chez la vieille dame. Le matin, avec elle, il fait de la gymnastique, puis il prend son bain.

Tous les jours il se promène en auto. C'est la vieille dame qui la lui a achetée. Elle lui donne tout ce qu'il veut.

Pourtant Babar n'est pas tout à fait heureux, car il ne peut plus jouer dans la grande forêt avec ses petits cousins et ses amis les singes.

Le récitant

Souvent, à la fenêtre, il rêve en pensant à son enfance

et pleure en se rappelant sa maman.

Deux années ont passé. Un jour pendant sa promenade, il voit venir à sa rencontre deux petits éléphants tout nus — "mais c'est Arthur et Céleste, mon petit cousin et ma cousine", dit-il, stupéfait, à la vieille dame.

Babar embrasse Arthur et Céleste, puis il va leur acheter de beaux costumes.

Follement gai et tumultueux ♩ = 88

Ensuite il les emmène chez le pâtissier manger de bons gâteaux.

Très gai et animé ie: I⁰ tempo ♩. = 100

Pendant ce temps, dans la forêt, les éléphants cherchent et appellent Arthur et Céleste, et leur mamans sont bien inquiètes.

Heureusement, en volant sur la ville, un vieux marabout les a vus. Vite il vient prévenir les éléphants.

Les mamans d'Arthur et de Céleste partent les chercher à la ville — elles sont bien contentes de les retrouver, mais elles les grondent tout de même parce qu'ils se sont sauvés.

THE STORY OF BABAR
the little elephant

Words by JEAN DE BRUNHOFF
English version by NELLY RIEU

Music by
FRANCIS POULENC

Note : The narrator will announce the title of the
work also the names of the Author and the Composer.
After a pause he will commence the recitation.

IN the great forest a little elephant was born. His name was Babar. His mother loved him dearly, and used to rock him to sleep with her trunk, singing to him softly the while.

Page 2, line 3. (18 bars)

Babar grew fast. Soon he was playing with the other baby elephants. He was one of the nicest of them. Look at him digging in the sand with a shell.

Page 4, line 3. (37 bars)

One day Babar was having a lovely ride on his Mother's back;

Page 5, line 1. (16 bars)

Suddenly a cruel hunter, hiding behind a bush, shot at them.

Page 5, line 2. (One bar)

The hunter killed Babar's mother. The monkey hid himself, the birds flew away. The hunter ran up to catch poor Babar. Babar was very frightened and ran away from the hunter.

Page 5, line 5. (11 bars)

After some days, tired and footsore, he came to a town. He was amazed, for it was the first time he had ever seen so many houses. What strange things he saw! Beautiful avenues! Motor cars and motor buses! But what interested Babar most of all was two gentlemen he met in the street. He thought to himself: "What lovely clothes they have got! I wish I could have some too! But how can I get them?"
Luckily, he was seen by a very rich old lady who understood little elephants, and knew at once that he was longing for a smart suit.
She loved making others happy, so she gave him her purse. "Thank you, Madam", said Babar.

Page 7, line 5. (28 bars)

Now Babar made his home in the old lady's house. Every morning they did their exercises together, and then Babar had his bath.

Page 9, line 1. (24 bars)

Every day he drove out in the car that the old lady had bought him. She gave him everything that he wanted.

Page 9, line 3. (5 bars)

And yet Babar was not altogether happy; he could no longer play about in the Great Forest with his little cousins and his friends the monkeys.

Note: This English version can be supplied to all Countries except the U.S.A. and Canada.
English Text by permission of Messrs. Methuen & Co. Ltd., London.
Music © copyright 1949, 1989 for all countries
Chester Music Ltd., 8/9 Frith Street, London W1V 5TZ

He often gazed out of the window, dreaming of his childhood . . .

a tempo

céder à peine

. . . And when he thought of his dear mother, . . . he used to cry.

a tempo

Page 10, *line* 4.   (10 *bars*)

Two years passed by. One day he was out for a walk when he met two little elephants with no clothes on. "Why, here are Arthur and Celeste, my two little cousins!" he cried in amazement to the old lady. Babar hugged Arthur and Celeste and took them to buy some lovely clothes.

Page 11, *line* 5.   (15 *bars*)

Next he took them to a tea-shop, where they had some delicious cakes.

Page 13, *line* 5.   (68 *bars*)

Meanwhile, in the Great Forest all the elephants were searching for Arthur and Celeste and their mothers grew more and more anxious.

Page 14, *line* 2.   (6 *bars*)

Luckily, an old bird flying over the town had spied them, and hurried back to tell the elephants.

Page 14, *line* 4.   (12 *bars*)

The mothers went to the town to fetch Arthur and Celeste. They were very glad when they found them, but they scolded them all the same for having run away.

Page 15, *line* 4.   (18 *bars*)

Babar made up his mind to return to the Great Forest with Arthur and Celeste and their mothers. When everything was ready for the journey Babar kissed his old friend good-bye. He promised to come back to her, and never to forget her. The old lady was left alone, sadly thinking; "When shall I see my little Babar again?"

Page 16, *line* 5.   (27 *bars*)

Off they went! There was no room for the mother elephants in the car! So they ran behind, lifting their trunks so as not to breathe in the dust.

Page 18, *line* 3.   (16 *bars*)

Alas! that very day the King of the elephants, during his walk, had eaten a bad mushroom.

Page 20, *line* 1.   (25 *bars*)

It had poisoned him. He had been very ill,

Page 20, *line* 2.   (2 *bars*)

So ill that he had died.

(4 *bars*)

It was a terrible misfortune.

Page 20, *line* 3.   (One *bar*)

After his funeral the oldest elephants met together to choose a new King. Just at that moment, they heard a noise and turned round. What a wonderful sight they saw! It was Babar arriving in his car, with all the elephants running and shouting: "Here they are! Here they are! They have come back! Hullo, Babar! Hullo, Arthur! Hullo, Celeste! What lovely clothes! What a beautiful car!"

Then Cornelius, the oldest elephant of all, said, in his quavering voice: "My dear friends, we must have a new King. Why not choose Babar? He has come back from the town, where he has lived among men and learnt much. Let us offer him the crown".

All the elephants thought that Cornelius had spoken wisely, and they listened eagerly to hear what Babar would say.

"I thank you all", said Babar: "but before accepting the crown I must tell you that on our journey in the car Celeste and I got engaged to be married. If I become your King, she will be your Queen".

"Long live Queen Celeste! Long live King Babar!" the elephants shouted with one voice.

And that was how Babar became . . . . King.

Page 22, line 5.   (*23 bars*)

"Cornelius", said Babar, "you have such good ideas that I shall make you a General, and when I get my crown I will give you my hat. In a week's time I am going to marry Celeste. We will give a grand party to celebrate our marriage and our coronation".

And Babar asked the birds to take invitations to all the animals.

Page 24, line 3.   (*29 bars*)

The guests began to arrive.

Page 24, line 5.   (*10 bars*)

The dromedary, who went to town to buy some fine wedding clothes . . . . .

. . . . Brought them just in time for the ceremony . . . .

surtout sans presser

Page 25, line 4.   (*6 bars*)

The Wedding of Babar.

Page 26, line 2.   (*7 bars*)

Babar's Coronation.

Page 27, line 2.   (*15 bars*)

After the wedding and the coronation everyone danced merrily.

Page 28, line 2.   (*16 bars*)

. . . . The birds sang with the orchestra . . . .

8ve   *Loco*

Page 29, line 3.   (*13 bars*)

The party was over.

Page 29, line 4.   (*One bar*)

Night fell . . . .

Le chant très lié et très doux ♩ = 66

Modéré

. . . . and the stars came out . . . .

ten.

Babar se décide à partir avec Arthur, Céleste et leur mamans et à revoir la grande forêt. Tout est prêt pour le départ. Babar embrasse sa vieille amie. Il lui promet de revenir — jamais il ne l'oubliera.

La vieille dame reste seule ; triste, elle pense : "Quand reverrai-je mon petit Babar?"

15

Ils sont partis . . . . Les mamans n'ont pas de place dans l'auto—elles courent derrière et lèvent leurs trompes pour ne pas respirer la poussière.

sans pédale

Le même jour, hélas, le roi des éléphants, au cours d'une promenade, a mangé un mauvais champignon.

Gracieux et modéré, avec précautions ♩ = 66

Empoisonné, il a été
bien malade. . . .

Si malade qu'il en est mort.

C'est un grand malheur.

Après l'enterrement les plus vieux des éléphants se sont réunis pour choisir un nouveau roi. Juste à ce moment ils entendent du bruit; il se retournent — qu'est ce qu'ils voient? Babar qui arrive dans son auto et tous les éléphants qui courent en criant: ''Les voilà! Les voilà! Ils sont revenus! Bonjour Babar! Bonjour Arthur! Bonjour Céleste! Quels beaux costumes! Quelle belle auto!'' Alors Cornélius, le plus vieux des éléphants dit, de sa voix tremblante:

''Mes bons amis, nous cherchons un roi, pourquoi ne pas choisir Babar? Il revient de la ville, il a beaucoup appris chez les hommes. Donnons lui la couronne.''

Tous les éléphants trouvent que Cornélius a très bien parlé. Impatients, ils attendent la réponse de Babar. ''Je vous remercie tous, dit alors ce dernier, mais avant d'accepter, je dois vous dire que, pendant notre voyage en auto, Céleste et moi nous nous sommes fiancés. Si je suis votre roi, elle sera votre reine.''

Vive la reine Céleste!! Vive le roi Babar!!! crient tous les éléphants sans hésiter.

Et c'est ainsi que

Babar devint . . . .

22

Babar dit alors à Cornélius: ''Tu as de bonnes idées, aussi je te nomme général et quand j'aurai
la couronne, je te donnerai mon chapeau melon. Dans huit jours j'épouserai Céleste; nous
aurons alors une grande fête pour notre mariage et notre couronnement.''
Ensuite Babar demande aux oiseaux d'aller inviter tous les animaux à ses noces.

Gai et très vif ♩ = 132

(*Le Récitant*)   Les invités commencent à arriver.

Le récitant

Le dromadaire, chargé d'acheter à la ville de beaux habits de noces, les rapporte

juste à temps pour le mariage.

surtout sans presser

(Le Récitant) Mariage de Babar.

Très lent et très pompeux ♩ = 60

(Le Récitant) Couronnement de Babar.

Après le mariage et le couronnement, tout le monde danse de bon coeur

28

(*Le Récitant*) Les oiseaux se mêlent à l'orchestre.

La fête est finie.

(Le Récitant) *(Très poétique et doux)*: La nuit est venue,

Le chant très lié et très doux ♩ = 66
Modéré

pp *Clair*

Baigné de pédales
(on n'en mettra jamais assez)

les étoiles se sont levées.   *ten.*

Le roi Babar et la reine Céleste
doucement ému

heureux . . . rêvent à leur bonheur.

Maintenant tout dort

les invités sont rentrés chez eux, très contents,

mais fatigués d'avoir trop dansé.

Longtemps ils se rappelleront ce grand bal.

Strictement en mesure

Paddington Bear's First Concert

Story by
Michael Bond

Music by
Herbert Chappell

arranged by the composer
for Narrator and Piano

Paddington, the lovable bear from Peru with a talent for trouble and a taste for marmalade sandwiches is famous around the world. Stories of his exploits have been translated into more than twenty languages. Already a star of stage and screen, he has now made his debut on the concert platform in Herbert Chappell's entertaining piece for narrator and orchestra: **Paddington Bear's First Concert.**

Michael Bond's story reminds us of Paddington's journey from Peru to the Portobello Road and some of the friends he found there. Its climax is reached with Paddington's unscheduled appearance mid-symphony on the platform of one of the world's great concert halls. Herbert Chappell's witty and attractive music illustrates the story aptly and its final pages give everyone the chance to join in with Paddington's own tune which is familiar as the theme music for the famous series of TV films which feature his adventures.

Paddington Bear's First Concert was a huge success at its first performance at a Barbican Teddy Bear's Concert in January 1986 and has proved equally popular at subsequent performances. This version for narrator and piano (specially arranged by the composer) can be used by narrators taking part in performances of the full orchestral version of the piece or for complete performances in halls, schools and at home where no symphony orchestra is available.

available from

CHESTER MUSIC
part of **WiseMusic**Group

EXCLUSIVELY DISTRIBUTED BY
 HAL•LEONARD®